Correlating Enhanced National Wetlands Inventory Data
with Wetland Functions for Watershed Assessments:
A Rationale for Northeastern U.S. Wetlands

Ralph W. Tiner
Regional Wetland Coordinator
U.S. Fish & Wildlife Service
Northeast Region
300 Westgate Center Drive
Hadley, MA 01035

October 2003

This publication should be cited as:

Tiner, R.W. 2003. Correlating Enhanced National Wetlands Inventory Data with Wetland Functions for Watershed Assessments: A Rationale for Northeastern U.S. Wetlands. U.S. Fish and Wildlife Service, National Wetlands Inventory Program, Region 5, Hadley, MA. 26 pp.

Table of Contents

Background

The U.S. Fish and Wildlife Service has been conducting the National Wetlands Inventory for over 25 years. The NWI Program has produced wetland maps for 91% (78% final) of the lower 48 states, all of Hawaii, and 35% of Alaska. Wetlands are classified according to the Service's official wetland classification system (Cowardin et al. 1979). This classification describes wetlands by ecological system (Marine, Estuarine, Lacustrine, Riverine, and Palustrine), by subsystem (e.g., water depth, exposure to tides), class (vegetative life form or substrate type), subclass, water regimes (hydrology), water chemistry (pH and salinity), and special modifiers (e.g., alterations by humans). The maps have been converted to digital data for 47% of the lower 48 states and 18% of Alaska. The availability of digital data and geographic information system (GIS) technology make it possible to use NWI data for various geospatial analyses.

In the 1990s, the NWI Program for the Northeast Region recognized the potential application of NWI data for watershed assessments, but realized that other attributes would have to be added to the data to facilitate functional analysis. Dr. Mark Brinson had recently developed a hydrogeomorphic (hgm) approach to wetland functional assessment (Brinson 1993a). This approach provided the impetus for developing other attributes to expand the NWI database and make it more useful for functional assessment.

In the mid-1990s, a set of hgm-type descriptors were developed to describe a wetland's landscape position, landform, and water flow path (Tiner 1995, 1996a,b). Use of the initial set of keys for pilot watershed projects lead to a refinement and expansion of the keys in subsequent years (Tiner 1997a, 2000, 2002, 2003). These projects were watershed characterizations that included a preliminary assessment of wetland functions as a main component or the prime component of the study. The reports addressed the following watersheds: Casco Bay (Maine; Tiner et al. 1999), Nanticoke River (Maryland and Delaware; Tiner et al. 2000, 2001), Coastal Bays (Maryland; Tiner et al. 2000), and Cannonsville and Neversink Reservoirs (New York; Tiner et al. 2002), as well as the Pennsylvania Coastal Zone (Tiner and DeAlessio 2002).

In conducting these studies, we worked with local and regional wetland experts to develop correlations between wetland characteristics recorded in the database and wetland functions (see Acknowledgments for listing). The correlations reflect our best approximation of what types of wetlands are likely to perform certain functions at significant levels based on the characteristics we have in the wetland database. Conducting wetland assessments in other areas, especially in arid, semiarid, and tropical regions, may identify other wetlands that need to be added to the significance list for various functions.

Limitations of the Preliminary Wetland Functional Assessment

Source data are a primary limiting factor. NWI digital data are used as the foundation for these assessments. In some cases, the NWI data are derived by updating more detailed state wetland data. Nonetheless, all wetland mapping has limitations due to scale, photo quality, date of the survey, and the difficulty of photointerpreting certain wetland types (especially evergreen forested wetlands and drier-end wetlands; see Tiner 1997c, 1999 for details).

Recognizing source data limitations, it is equally important to understand that this type of functional assessment is a preliminary one based on wetland characteristics interpreted through remote sensing and using the best professional judgment of various specialists to develop correlations between wetland characteristics in the database and wetland functions. Also, no attempt is made to produce a more qualitative ranking for each function or for each wetland based on multiple functions as this would require more input from others and more data, well beyond the scope of this type of evaluation. For a technical review of wetland functions, see Mitsch and Gosselink (2000) and for a broad overview, see Tiner (1998).

Functional assessment of wetlands can involve many parameters. Typically such assessments have been done in the field on a case-by-case basis, considering observed features relative to those required to perform certain functions or by actual measurement of performance. The preliminary assessments based on remotely sensed information do not seek to replace the need for field evaluations since they represent the ultimate assessment of the functions for individual wetlands. Yet, for a watershed analysis, basin-wide field-derived assessments are not practical, cost-effective, or even possible given access considerations. For watershed planning purposes, a more generalized assessment (level 1 assessment) is worthwhile for targeting wetlands that may provide certain functions, especially for those functions dependent on landscape position, landform, hydrologic processes, and vegetative life form. Subsequently, these results can be field-verified when it comes to actually evaluating particular wetlands for acquisition purposes (e.g., for conserving biodiversity or for preserving flood storage capacity) or for project impact assessment. Current aerial photography may also be examined to aid in further evaluations (e.g., condition of wetland/stream buffers or adjacent land use) that can supplement the preliminary assessment.

The functional assessment approach -"Watershed-based Preliminary Assessment of Wetland Functions" (W-PAWF) - applies general knowledge about wetlands and their functions to develop a watershed overview that highlights possible wetlands of significance in terms of performance of various functions. To accomplish this objective, the relationships between wetlands and various functions are simplified into a set of practical criteria or observable characteristics. Such assessments may be further expanded to consider the condition of the associated waterbody and the neighboring upland or to evaluate the opportunity a wetland has to perform a particular function or service to society, for example.

W-PAWF usually does not account for the opportunity that a wetland has to provide a function resulting from a certain land-use practice upstream or the presence of certain structures or land-uses downstream. For example, two wetlands of equal size and like vegetation may be in the right landscape position to retain sediments. One, however, may be downstream of a land-clearing operation that has generated considerable suspended sediments in the water column, while the other is downstream from an undisturbed forest. The former should be actively performing sediment trapping in a major way, whereas the latter is not. Yet if land-clearing takes place in the latter area, the second wetland will likely trap sediments as well as the first wetland. The entire analysis typically tends to ignore opportunity since such opportunity may have occurred in the past or may occur in the future and the wetland is there to perform this service at higher levels when necessary.

W-PAWF also does not consider the condition of the adjacent upland (e.g., level of disturbance) or the actual water quality of the associated waterbody that may be regarded as important metrics for assessing the health of individual wetlands. Collection and analysis of these data may be done as a followup investigation, where desired.

It is important re-emphasize that the preliminary assessment does not obviate the need for more detailed assessments of the various functions. This type of assessment should be viewed as a starting point for more rigorous assessments, since it attempts to cull out wetlands that may likely provide significant functions based on generally accepted principles and the source information used for this analysis. This assessment is most useful for regional or watershed planning purposes. For site-specific evaluations, additional work will be required, especially field verification and collection of site-specific data for potential functions (e.g., following the HGM assessment approach as described by Brinson 1993a or other onsite evaluation procedures). This is particularly true for assessments of fish and wildlife habitats and biodiversity. Other sources of data may exist to help refine some of the findings of this report (e.g., state natural heritage data). Additional modeling could be done, for example, to identify habitats of likely significance to individual species of animals based on their specific life history requirements (see U.S. Fish and Wildlife Service 2003 for Gulf of Maine habitat analysis).

Also note that the criteria used for the correlations were based on regional application of the Service's wetland classification (Cowardin et al. 1979). Regional applications of this system may differ slightly depending on regional priorities, level of field effort, and knowledge of wetland ecology. Use of the correlations in other regions of the country therefore may require some adjustment based on these considerations.

Through this analysis, numerous wetlands are predicted to perform a given function at a significant level presumably important to a watershed's ability to provide that function. "Significance" is a relative term and is used in this analysis to identify wetlands that are likely to perform a given function at a level above that of wetlands not designated. It is also emphasized that the assessment is limited to wetlands (i.e., areas classified as wetlands on NWI maps or similar sources). Deepwater habitats and streams were not included in the assessment, although their inherent value to wetlands and many wetland-dependent organisms is apparent.

Rationale for Preliminary Functional Assessments

A maximum of ten functions may be evaluated: 1) surface water detention, 2) coastal storm surge detention, 3) streamflow maintenance, 4) nutrient transformation, 5) sediment and other particulate retention, 6) shoreline stabilization, 7) provision of fish and shellfish habitat, 8) provision of waterfowl and waterbird habitat, 9) provision of other wildlife habitat, and 10) conservation of biodiversity. The criteria used for identifying wetlands of significance for these functions using the digital wetland database are discussed below. The criteria were initially developed by the author of this report based on his knowledge of wetland characteristics and functions. The draft criteria were then reviewed and modified for the subject watersheds based on comments from wetland specialists working on specific watersheds in four Northeast states (Maine, New York, Delaware, and Maryland). (Note: Criteria may need to be modified for other regions of the country, although many are universally applicable.)

In developing a protocol for designating wetlands of potential significance, wetland size was generally disregarded from the criteria, with few exceptions (i.e., other wildlife habitat and biodiversity functions). This approach was followed because it was felt that individual agencies and organizations using the digital database and charged with setting priorities should make the decision on appropriate size criteria as a means of limiting the number of priority wetlands, if necessary. There is no science-based size limit to establish significance for any function. However, it is obvious that, all things being equal, a larger wetland will have a higher capacity to perform a given function than a smaller one of the same type. The W-PAWF approach is intended to produce a more expansive characterization of wetlands and their likely functions and not to develop a rapid assessment method for ranking wetlands for acquisition, protection, or other purposes.

The criteria for identifying different levels of potential significance can be modified in the future based on additional peer review, application to other watersheds and regions, and field evaluation. The proposed criteria are designed for wetlands in the Northeast, but many, if not most, should be relevant nationwide. Some of the criteria, especially those addressing fish and wildlife habitat, will need to be re-examined for individual watersheds, particularly when this approach is applied to other regions of the country. Note that palustrine farmed wetlands have not been identified as being significant for any function in the Northeast. Since they are tilled cropland or cultivated cranberry bogs, farmed wetlands were viewed as severely degraded wetlands that perform the specified functions at minimal levels. Consequently, they represented sites where substantial gains in wetland functions may be achieved through restoration projects. In other parts of the country, farmed wetlands may perform some wetland functions at significant levels (e.g., farmed pothole wetlands in the Midwest or diked former tidelands in the Sacramento River valley - important waterfowl habitat).

Surface Water Detention

This function is important for reducing downstream flooding and lowering flood heights, both of which aid in minimizing property damage and personal injury from such events. In a landmark study on the relationships between wetlands and flooding at the watershed scale, Novitzki (1979) found that watersheds with 40 percent coverage by lakes and wetlands had significantly reduced flood flows -- lowered by as much as 80 percent -- compared to similar watersheds with no or few lakes and wetlands in Wisconsin. Floodplain wetlands, other lotic wetlands (basin and flat types), estuarine fringe wetlands along coastal rivers, and estuarine island wetlands in these rivers provide this function at significant levels. At the present time, estuarine and marine rocky shores are rated as high for this function, since they are usually narrow habitats and/or intermixed with tidal flats. Perhaps this function should be limited to non-estuarine habitats, with the water storage function of estuarine wetlands listed under coastal storm surge detention and shoreline stabilization. Presently, estuarine and marine wetlands are recognized as important areas for storing surface water, recognizing that it is tidal water that ebbs and flows.

Wetlands dominated by trees and/or dense stands of shrubs could be deemed to provide a higher level of this function than emergent wetlands, since woody vegetation (with higher frictional resistance) may further aid in flood desynchronization. However, emergent wetlands along waterways provide significant flood storage, so no distinction is made regarding the type of vegetative cover. Floodplain width could also be an important factor in evaluating the significance of performance of this function by individual wetlands (e.g., for acquisition or strengthened protection), but there is no scientifically based criterion for establishing a significance threshold based on size.

Interfluve wetlands and drier-end wetlands (e.g., Lotic Flats) are rated as having moderate potential. While Interfluve basins hold more water than Interfluve flats, no distinction was made since they represent a single system that tends to be dominated by flats. Wetland size was not considered, but it is obvious that size should make a difference in the amount of water stored. Others interested in prioritizing wetlands for acquisition or protection may wish to identify a minimum threshold for importance for this function or develop other criteria for prioritization (e.g., treat small interfluve flats differently from small interfluve basins).

For this function, the following correlations are used:

> High   Estuarine Fringe, Estuarine Basin, Estuarine Island, Lentic Basin, Lentic Fringe, Lentic Island (basin and fringe), Lentic Flat associated with reservoirs and flood control dams, Lotic Basin, Lotic Floodplain, Lotic Fringe, Lotic Island associated with Floodplain area, Lotic Island basin, Marine Fringe, Marine Island, Ponds   Throughflow
>
> (in-
>
> stream) and associated Fringe and Basin wetlands, Ponds Bidirectional and associated wetlands, Terrene Throughflow Basin

Moderate	Lotic Flat, Lotic Island flat, Lentic Flat, Terrene Interfluve, Other Terrene Basins, Other Ponds and associated wetlands (excluding sewage treatment ponds and similar waters)

Coastal Storm Surge Detention

This function is listed separately from Surface Water Detention to highlight the importance of tidal wetlands at storing tidal waters brought into estuaries by storms (e.g., Nor'easters, tropical storms, and hurricanes). Estuarine and freshwater tidal wetlands are important areas for temporary storage of this water. At the present time, estuarine and marine rocky shores that are fringe types are rated as high for this function, since they are usually narrow habitats and/or intermixed with tidal flats. Some nontidal wetlands contiguous to these wetlands (e.g., low-lying terrene outflow basins - flatwoods) may also provide this function, but it was not possible to predict the extent of such storage as this depends on storm intensity and frequency.

For this function, the following correlations are used:

High	Estuarine Basin, Estuarine Fringe, Estuarine Island, Lotic Tidal Fringe, Lotic Tidal Island, Lotic Tidal Floodplain, Marine Fringe

Streamflow Maintenance

Many wetlands are sources of groundwater discharge and some may be in a position to sustain streamflow in the watershed. Such wetlands are critically important for supporting aquatic life in streams. All wetlands classified as headwater wetlands are important for streamflow (e.g, Terrene headwater wetlands, by definition, are sources of streams). These wetlands include lotic wetlands along 1st-order streams and lentic wetlands associated with outflow lakes. Wetlands along 2nd-order streams in mountainous areas may be classified as headwater wetlands as they probably are sites of groundwater discharge. Ditched headwater wetlands are rated as "Moderate," since this alteration typically results in faster release of water, thereby reducing the period of outflow. Outflow from groundwater-fed wetlands (lacking a stream) may discharge directly into streams and thereby contribute substantial quantities of water for sustaining baseflows. These wetlands were rated as "Moderate" for this function. Lakes may also be important regulators of streamflow, so lentic wetlands may be designated as significant to streamflow, with those in headwater positions being rated "High" and others as "Moderate."

Floodplain wetlands are known to store water in the form of bank storage, later releasing this water to maintain baseflows (Whiting 1998). Among several key factors affecting bank storage are porosity and permeability of the bank material, the width of the floodplain, and the hydraulic gradient (steepness of the water table). The wider the floodplain, the more bank storage given the same soils. Gravel floodplains drain in days, sandy floodplains in a few weeks to a few years, silty floodplains in years, and clayey floodplains in decades. In good water years, wide sandy floodplains may help maintain baseflows. Despite these differences, the W-PAWF

6

assessment treats all floodplain wetlands similarly, since it is based on remote sensing and does not include soil examinations.

For this function, the following correlations are used:

High	Nonditched Headwater Wetlands (Terrene, Lotic, and Lentic), Headwater Ponds and Lakes (classified as PUB...on NWI) (Note: Lotic Stream Basin or Floodplain basin Wetlands along 2nd order streams should also be rated high; possibly expand to 3rd order streams in hilly or mountainous terrain.)
Moderate	Ditched Headwater Wetlands (Terrene, Lotic, and Lentic), Lotic (Nontidal) Floodplain, Throughflow Ponds and Lakes (classified as PUB on NWI) and their associated wetlands, Terrene Outflow wetlands (associated with streams not major rivers), Outflow Ponds and Lakes (classified as PUB... on NWI)

Special Note: All these wetlands should be considered to also be important for fish and shellfish as they are vital to sustaining streamflow necessary for the survival of these aquatic organisms.

Nutrient Transformation

All wetlands recycle nutrients, but those having a fluctuating water table are best able to recycle nitrogen and other nutrients. Vegetation slows the flow of water causing deposition of mineral and organic particles with adsorbed nutrients (nitrogen and phosphorus), whereas hydric soils are the places where chemical transformations occur (Carter 1996). Microbial action in the soil is the driving force behind chemical transformations in wetlands. Microbes need a food source -- organic matter -- to survive, so wetlands with high amounts of organic matter should have an abundance of microflora to perform the nutrient cycling function. Wetlands are so effective at filtering and transforming nutrients that artificial wetlands are constructed for water quality renovation (e.g., Hammer 1992). Natural wetlands performing this function help improve local water quality of streams and other watercourses.

Numerous studies have demonstrated the importance of wetlands in denitrification. Simmons et al. (1992) found high nitrate removal (greater than 80%) from groundwater during both the growing season and dormant season in Rhode Island streamside (lotic) wetlands. Groundwater temperatures throughout the dormant season were between 6.5 and 8.0 degrees C, so microbial activity was not limited by temperature. Even the nearby upland, especially transitional areas with somewhat poorly drained soils, experienced an increase in nitrogen removal during the dormant season. This was attributed to a seasonal rise in the water table that exposed the upper portion of the groundwater to soil with more organic matter (nearer the ground surface), thereby supporting microbial activity and denitrification. Riparian forests dominated by wetlands have a greater proportion of groundwater (with nitrate) moving within the biologically active zone of the soil that makes nitrate susceptible to uptake by plants and microbes (Nelson et al. 1995). Riparian forests on well-drained soils are much less effective at removing nitrate. In a Rhode Island study, Nelson et al. (1995) found that November had the highest nitrate removal rate due to the highest water tables in the poorly drained soils, while June experienced the lowest removal rate when the deepest water table levels occurred. Similar results can be expected to occur elsewhere. For bottomland hardwood wetlands, DeLaune et al. (1996) reported decreases in nitrate from 59-82 percent after 40 days of flooding wetland soil cores taken from the Cache River floodplain in Arkansas. Moreover, they surmised that denitrification in these soils appeared to be carbon-limited: increased denitrification took place in soils with more organic matter in the surface layer.

Nitrogen fixation is accomplished in wetlands by microbial-driven reduction processes that convert nitrate to nitrogen gas. Nitrogen removal rates for freshwater wetlands are very high (averaging from 20-80 grams/square meter) (Bowden 1987). The following information comes from a review paper on this topic by Buresh et al. (1980). Nitrogen fixation has been attributed to blue-green algae in the photic zone at the soil-water interface and to heterotrophic bacteria associated with plant roots. In working with rice, Matsuguchi (1979) believed that the significance of heterotrophic fixation in the soil layer beyond the roots has been underrated and presented data showing that such zones were the most important sites for nitrogen fixation in a Japanese rice field. This conclusion was further supported by Wada et al. (1978). Higher fixation rates have been found in the rhizosphere of wetland plants than in dryland plants.

Phosphorus removal is largely done by plant uptake (Patrick, undated manuscript). Wetlands that accumulate peat have a great capacity for phosphorus removal. Wetland drainage can, therefore, change a wetland from a phosphorus sink to a phosphorus source. This is a significant cause of water quality degradation in many areas of the world including the United States, where wetlands are drained for agricultural production. Hydric soils with significant clay constituents fix phosphorus due to its interaction with clay and inorganic colloids. Reduced soils have more sorption sites than oxidized soils (Patrick and Khalid 1974), while the latter soils have stronger bonding energy and adsorb phosphorus more tightly.

From the water quality standpoint, wetlands associated with watercourses are probably the most noteworthy. Numerous studies have found that forested wetlands along rivers and streams (Ariparian forested wetlands@) are important for nutrient retention and sedimentation during floods (Whigham et al. 1988; Yarbro et al. 1984; Simpson et al. 1983; Peterjohn and Correll 1982). This function by forested riparian wetlands is especially important in agricultural areas. Brinson (1993b) suggests that riparian wetlands along low-order streams may be more important than those along higher order streams.

Wetlands with seasonally flooded and wetter water regimes (including tidal regimes - seasonally flooded-tidal, irregularly flooded, and regularly flooded) are identified as having potential to recycle nutrients at high levels of performance. The soils of these wetlands should have substantial amounts of organic matter near the surface that promote microbial activity and denitrification when wet. Based on field observations, in general, there is a positive correlation between the amount of organic matter and the degree of wetness as reflected by the NWI's water regime classification in wetlands of the Nanticoke River watershed in Delaware (Amy Jacobs, pers. comm. 2003). Periodically flooded soils also retain sediments and their adsorbed nutrients.

Seasonally saturated wetlands are also rated as having high potential for this function. Most the the groundwater flux from uplands to surface waters occurs in the non-growing season in the Northeast and reasonable denitrification rates occur in spring and fall making sites that are wet during these times important for nutrient retention (Art Gold, pers. comm. 2003). Permanently saturated wetlands in nutrient-rich sites should also be rated as high for this function, whereas wetlands with this hydrology in nutrient-poor areas are rated as moderate. The latter types are nutrient-deficient habitats, yet they may have considerable potential for nutrient uptake should more nutrients become available due to land use practices.

Wetlands with a temporarily flooded water regime including those in tidal environments (temporarily flooded-tidal) are identified as having a moderate potential for performing this function. Vegetated wetlands with a seasonally saturated water regime are also considered as moderate, since they are usually wet longer during the non-growing season and for shorter periods during the growing season.

Drainage through ditches or tiles can significantly reduce nutrient transformation by lowering the water table below the zone of highest biological activity (Art Gold, pers. comm. 2003). Partly drained wetlands that are listed as having wetter water regimes (i.e., C, E and F) should still perform this function significantly (i.e., like their nondrained counterparts) since this function appears positively correlated with water regime. Drained wetlands on the drier-end of the soil moisture gradient (i.e., A and B water regimes) likely perform this function to a less degree and are therefore rated as having moderate potential.

For this function, correlations are the following:

High	Vegetated wetlands (and mixes with nonvegetated wetlands or unconsolidated bottom; even where nonvegetated predominates) with seasonally flooded (C), seasonally flooded/saturated (E), semipermanently flooded (F), semipermanently flooded-tidal (T), seasonally flooded-tidal (R), irregularly flooded (P), regularly flooded (N), and permanently flooded (H or L) water regimes, vegetated wetlands with <u>permanently saturated</u> water regime (B; *not on the coastal plain or glaciolacustrine plains*).
Moderate	Vegetated wetlands with <u>seasonally saturated</u> (B *on the coastal plain and on glaciolacustrine plains*, e.g., Great Lakes Plain in western New York), temporarily flooded (A) or temporarily flooded-tidal (S) water regimes

Retention of Sediments and Other Particulates

Many wetlands owe their existence to being located in areas of sediment deposition. This is especially true for floodplain and estuarine wetlands. This function supports water quality maintenance by capturing sediments with bonded nutrients or heavy metals (as in and downstream of urban areas). Estuarine and floodplain wetlands plus lotic (streamside) and lentic (lakeshore) fringe and basin wetlands including lotic (in-stream) ponds are likely to trap and retain sediments and particulates at significant levels. Terrene throughflow basins should function similarly. Vegetated wetlands will likely favor sedimentation over nonvegetated wetlands and are therefore rated higher. Lotic flat wetlands are flooded only for brief periods and less frequently than the wetlands listed above due to their elevation; they are classified as having moderate potential for sediment retention. Throughflow (in-stream) ponds are rated as "High," since they occur within the stream network. Other ponds may be locally significant in retaining such materials, and are also designated as "Moderate." Interfluve flats are not rated as potentially significant because they are level landscapes that do not appear to accumulate substantial amounts of sediment from surrounding areas, whereas Interfluve basins are depressional landscapes that likely collect sediments. The latter wetlands were rated as having moderate potential. Bogs and rocky shores are not considered significant sites for sediment retention and are therefore excluded from the list. Wetlands that are not flooded (e.g., seasonally saturated flatwoods) are also not considered to perform this function at significant levels.

For this function, the following correlations are used:

High — Estuarine Basin (vegetated), Estuarine Fringe (vegetated excluding rocky shores), Estuarine Island (vegetated), Lentic Basin, Lentic Fringe (vegetated only), Lentic Island (vegetated) Lotic Basin, Lotic Floodplain, Lotic Fringe (vegetated), Lotic Island (vegetated), Throughflow Ponds and Lakes (in-stream; designated as PUB... on NWI) and associated vegetated wetlands, Bidirectional Ponds and associated vegetated wetlands, Terrene Throughflow Basin and Interfluve Basin

Moderate — Estuarine Basin (nonvegetated), Estuarine Fringe (nonvegetated excluding rocky shore), Estuarine Island (nonvegetated, excluding rocky shore), Lotic Island (nonvegetated), Lotic Flat (excluding bogs), Lotic Tidal Fringe (nonvegetated), Lentic Flat, Marine Fringe (excluding rocky shore), Marine Island (excluding rocky shore), Other Terrene Basins (excluding bogs), Other Terrene Interfluve Basins, Terrene wetlands associated with ponds (excluding excavated ponds; also excluding bogs and slope wetlands), Other Ponds and Lakes (classified as PUB... on NWI) and associated wetlands (excluding bogs and slope wetlands)
(Note: Users might want to considerremoving certain types of ponds from this category, such as ponds with minimal watersheds - possibly gravel pit ponds, impoundments

completely surrounded by dikes, and dug-out ponds with little surface water inflow.)

Shoreline Stabilization

Vegetated wetlands along all waterbodies (e.g., estuaries, lakes, rivers, and streams) provide this function. Vegetation stabilizes the soil or substrate and diminishes wave action, thereby reducing shoreline erosion potential. There is less wave or erosive action along pond shores, so vegetated shoreline wetlands along ponds are designated as "Moderate." Marine and estuarine rocky shores form stable shorelines in several parts of the country. Consequently, they are rated as "High" for this function, except where these wetland types are islands that are inundated completely at times. In the latter situation, they are not shoreline features fringing an upland.

For this function, the following correlations are used:

> High — Estuarine wetlands (vegetated except island types), Estuarine Rocky Shore (excluding island types), Marine Rocky Shore (excluding island types), Lotic wetlands (vegetated except island and isolated types), Lentic wetlands (vegetated except island types)

> Moderate — Terrene vegetated wetlands associated with ponds (e.g., Fringe-pond, Flat-pond, and Basin-pond)

Provision of Fish and Shellfish Habitat[1]

The assessment of potential habitat for fish and shellfish is based on generalities that could be refined for particular species of interest by others at a later date if desireable. Regional and local variations will need to be accounted for on a watershed-by-watershed basis. The criteria selected below are useful for the Northeast and many may be applicable nationwide, but they should be re-examined for each project watershed to ensure accuracy and completeness. Although focused on fish and shellfish, wetlands identified as significant for these species are likely also significant for other aquatic-dependent species such as muskrat, turtles, and numerous frogs.

For tidal areas, the assessment emphasizes palustrine and riverine tidal emergent wetlands, unconsolidated shores (tidal flats), and estuarine wetlands. For nontidal regions, palustrine aquatic beds and semipermanently flooded wetlands are ranked higher than seasonally flooded types due to the longer duration of surface water. Palustrine forested wetlands along streams (lotic stream wetlands) are recognized as important for maintaining fish and shellfish habitat since their canopies help moderate water temperatures and their leaf litter provides food for aquatic organisms (e.g., aquatic invertebrates) that sustain juvenile and some adult fishes. Many ponds (excluding wastewater ponds, for example) and the shallow marsh-open water zone of

---

[1] This assessment is focused on wetlands, not deepwater habitats, hence the exclusion of the latter from this analysis, despite widespread recognition that rivers, streams, ponds, and impoundments are the primary habitats for fish and shellfish.

impoundments are identified as wetlands having moderate potential for fish and shellfish habitat. Those associated with semipermanently flooded wetlands were listed as "High" since they are important nursery grounds and feeding grounds for adults of some species.

Other wetlands providing significant fish habitat may exist, but are not identified. Such wetlands may be identified based on actual observations or culled out from site-specific fisheries information that may be available from other sources. Moreover, all wetlands that are significant for the streamflow maintenance function could be considered vital to sustaining the watershed's ability to provide in-stream fish and shellfish habitat. While these wetlands may not be providing significant fish and shellfish habitat themselves, they support base flows essential to keeping water in streams for aquatic life. Terrene outflow wetlands and Lotic basin wetlands along low order streams (e.g., orders 1-2 in Coastal Plain and 1-3 in hilly or mountainous terrain) often discharge cool groundwater to streams which keeps these streams cooler in summer. Such wetlands are important for providing summer refuges for trout and other coldwater species, especially in warm climate regions (Francis Brautigam, pers. comm. 2003). Other wetlands along waterbodies provide food that supports aquatic organisms that are an important part of the diet of juvenile and some adult fishes.

For this function, the following correlations are used:

High   Estuarine Emergent Wetland (including mixtures with other types where Emergent is the dominant class), Estuarine Unconsolidated Shore, Estuarine Intertidal Reef, Estuarine Aquatic Bed, Estuarine Intertidal Rocky Shore, Lacustrine Semipermanently Flooded (excluding wetlands along intermittent streams), Lacustrine Littoral Aquatic Bed, Lacustrine Littoral Unconsolidated Bottom/Vegetated Wetland, Lacustrine Littoral Vegetated Wetland with a Permanently Flooded water regime, Marine Aquatic Bed, Marine Intertidal Rocky Shore, Marine Intertidal Unconsolidated Shore, Marine Intertidal Reef, Palustrine Semipermanently Flooded (excluding wetlands along intermittent streams; *must be contiguous with a permanent waterbody* such as PUBH, L1UBH, or R2/R3UBH), Palustrine Aquatic Bed, Palustrine Unconsolidated Bottom/Vegetated Wetland, Palustrine Vegetated Wetland with a Permanently Flooded water regime, Palustrine Tidal Emergent Wetland with N, R, T, or L water regimes (excluding "R" wetlands where EM5 is only dominant), Ponds (PUBH.. on NWI; not PUBF) associated with Semipermanently Flooded Vegetated Wetland, Riverine Tidal Emergent Wetland, Riverine Tidal Unconsolidated Shore (excluding those with an "S" water regime)

Moderate   Estuarine Wetlands where Forested or Scrub-Shrub Wetland is mixed with Emergent Wetland, Palustrine Tidal Forested or Scrub-Shrub Wetland mixed with Emergent Wetland having a

R or T water regime, Lentic wetlands that are PEM1E, Lotic River or Stream wetlands that are PEM1E (including mixtures with Scrub-Shrub or Forested wetlands), Semipermanently flooded <u>Phragmites</u> wetlands (PEM5F) where contiguous with a permanent waterbody, Other Ponds and associated Fringe wetlands (i.e., Terrene Fringe-pond) (excluding industrial, stormwater treatment/detention, similar ponds in highly disturbed landscapes, and ponds with K and F water regimes)

Important for Stream Shading
Lotic Stream wetlands that are Palustrine Forested or Scrub-shrub wetlands (includes mixes where one of these types predominates; excluding those along intermittent streams; also excluding shrub bogs) (*Note that although forested wetlands are designated as important for stream shading, forested upland provide similar functions*)

Local
Lake Champlain example: Seasonally flooded Lentic wetlands (along Lake Champlain - important spawning areas in spring)

Provision of Waterfowl and Waterbird Habitat

Wetlands designated as important for waterfowl (e.g., ducks, geese, mergansers, and loons) and waterbirds (e.g., wading birds, shorebirds, rails, marsh wrens, and red-winged blackbirds) are generally those used for nesting, reproduction, or feeding. The emphasis is on the wetter wetlands and ones that are frequently flooded for long periods. The criteria for selection should be re-examined for each watershed as there may be regional and local differences in habitat requirements that need to be accounted for. The criteria listed below should, however, be useful for most of the country.

The selected wetlands include estuarine wetlands (vegetated or not), riverine emergent wetlands, estuarine and riverine unconsolidated shores (excluding temporary flooded-tidal), palustrine tidal and riverine tidal emergent wetlands (including emergent/shrub mixtures), semipermanently flooded wetlands, mixed open water-emergent wetlands (palustrine and lacustrine), and aquatic beds. Marine rocky shores are rated as having "High" since sea ducks, mergansers, and loons feed extensively in such areas (George Haas, pers. comm. 2003). <u>Phragmites</u>-dominated wetlands are listed as "Moderate" when they are contiguous to a permanent waterbody; those that are flooded either regularly flooded (N) in tidal areas or semipermanently flooded (F) in nontidal areas are designated as "High" since they provide excellent escape cover and night roosting cover (George Haas, pers. comm. 2003). For this analysis, palustrine tidal scrub-shrub/emergent wetlands and tidal forested/emergent wetlands were designated as having moderate significance for these birds. Similar mixed wetlands dominated by emergent species, however, are listed as having high significance, since the emergents typically represent wetter conditions. Ponds were considered to have moderate potential for providing waterfowl and waterbird habitat.[2] <u>Phragmites</u>-dominated wetlands were listed as having moderate potential for they receive some use by waterfowl and waterbirds.

Other wetlands that may be significant principally for wood duck are identified. Since wooded streams are particularly important for them, seasonally flooded lotic wetlands that are forested or mixtures of trees and shrubs (excluding those along intermittent streams) are designated as wetlands with significant potential for use by this species. Similar seasonally flooded-tidal wetlands bordering oligohaline estuarine wetlands may also be important for wood duck as well as for providing shelter from winter storms for overwintering black ducks. Recognize that wetlands listed as having high potential for waterfowl and waterbird habitat also include some types important to wood ducks (e.g., semipermanently flooded lotic shrub/emergent wetlands); their value to wood ducks has not been highlighted given that they were already designated as having high potential for waterfowl and waterbirds.

Seasonally flooded emergent wetlands (including mixtures with shrubs) were not designated as potentially significant for waterfowl and waterbirds. Field checking of these types may reveal that some are freshwater marshes that provide significant habitat; they should then be added to database as wetlands of significance for this function. Although palustrine forested wetlands along freshwater tidal rivers and streams were designated as important for wood duck, similar wetland behind estuarine wetlands were not identified as significant. These wetlands need further evaluation by local waterfowl experts as we recognize that forested wetlands provide important shelter for overwintering black ducks during coastal storm events, but are uncertain as to the role played by this subset of forested wetlands.

For this function, the following correlations were used:

High   Estuarine Aquatic Bed, Estuarine Emergent wetlands (excluding Phragmites-dominated wetlands; including mixtures with other vegetated types, e.g., EM/SS), Estuarine Unconsolidated Shore (except S water regime), Estuarine Intertidal Reef, Lacustrine Semipermanently Flooded, Lacustrine Littoral Aquatic Bed, Lacustrine Littoral Vegetated wetlands with an H water regime, Lacustrine Unconsolidated Shores (F, E, or C water regimes; mudflats), Marine Aquatic Bed, Marine Intertidal Reef, Marine Unconsolidated Shore, Marine Rocky Shores, Palustrine Semipermanently Flooded and Semipermanently Flooded-Tidal (excluding Phragmites stands, but including mixtures containing this species - EM5), Palustrine Aquatic Bed, Palustrine Vegetated wetlands with a H water regime,

---

[2]Ponds on wildlife management areas (e.g., refuges) should be considered to be of high significance due to their management. Since we do not presently have the location of refuges recorded in our digital database, these ponds may not be separated from the rest of the ponds. Hence, all ponds except industrial, commercial, stormwater detention, wastewater treatment, and similar ponds, are designated as having moderate potential for this function.

Palustrine Unconsolidated Shores (F, E, or C water regimes; mudflats), Seasonally Flooded/Saturated Palustrine wetlands impounded or beaver-influenced (all vegetation types [except PEM5Eh and PEM5Eb] and associated PUB waters), Lotic River or Stream wetlands that are PEM1E (including mixtures with Scrub-Shrub or Forested wetlands), Ponds associated with Semipermanently Flooded Vegetated wetlands, Palustrine Tidal Emergent wetlands (PEM1R and PEM1T and mixes with other EM and with SS and FO; excluding wetlands where EM5 is the only EM), Riverine Tidal Emergent wetlands, Riverine Tidal Unconsolidated Shores (except with S water regime), Ponds associated with all of the above wetland types

Moderate   Phragmites wetlands that are Seasonally Flooded/Saturated and wetter (PEM5E; PEM5F; PEM5H, and PEM5R) *and* contiguous with a waterbody, Phragmites-dominated Estuarine Emergent wetlands *and* contiguous to a waterbody, Seasonally Flooded-Tidal Palustrine Wetland where EM is the subordinate mixed class (e.g., PFO1/EM1R), Other Lacustrine Littoral Unconsolidated Bottom, Other Palustrine Unconsolidated Bottom (excluding industrial, commercial, stormwater detention, wastewater treatment, and similar ponds), Palustrine Emergent wetlands (including mixtures with Scrub-shrub) that are Seasonally Flooded and associated with permanently flooded waterbodies

Significant for
Wood Duck   Lotic wetlands (excluding those along intermittent streams) that are Forested or Scrub-shrub or mixtures of these types with C, E, F, R, or H water regime; Lotic wetlands that are mixed Forested/Emergent or Unconsolidated Bottom/Forested with a E, F, R, or H water regime; Palustrine Tidal Forested or Scrub-shrub wetlands (and mixes with other types like the Lotic types) in estuarine reach with R or L water regime

Provision of Other Wildlife Habitat

The provision of other wildlife habitat by wetlands was evaluated in general terms. Species-specific habitat requirements were not considered. The criteria listed below are designed for the Northeast and many should be useful nationwide, but habitat requirements for regional and local wildlife need to be considered on a watershed-by-watershed basis for best results.

15

In developing an evaluation method for wildlife habitat in the glaciated Northeast, Golet (1972) designated several types as outstanding wildlife wetlands including: 1) wetlands with rare, restricted, endemic, or relict flora and/or fauna, 2) wetlands with unusually high visual quality and infrequent occurrence, 3) wetlands with flora and fauna at the limits of their range, 4) wetlands with several seral stages of hydrarch succession, and 5) wetlands used by great numbers of migratory waterfowl, shorebirds, marsh birds, and wading birds. Golet subscribed to the principle that in general, as wetland size increases so does wildlife value, so wetland size was important factor for determining wildlife habitat potential in his approach. Other important variables included dominant wetland class, site type (bottomland vs. upland; associated with waterbody vs. isolated), surrounding habitat type (e.g., natural vegetation vs. developed land), degree of interspersion (water vs. vegetation), wetland juxtaposition (proximity to other wetlands), and water chemistry.

For this analysis, wetlands important to waterfowl and waterbirds are identified in a separate assessment (see above) and rare wetlands are addressed in the function called "conservation of biodiversity" (see following subsection). Emphasis for assessing "other wildlife" was placed on conditions that would likely provide significant habitat for other vertebrate wildlife (mainly herps, interior forest birds, and mammals). Opportunistic species that are highly adaptable to fragmented landscapes are not among the target organisms, since there seems to be more than ample habitat for these species now and in the future. Rather, animals whose populations may decline as wetland habitats become fragmented by development are of key concern. For example, breeding success of neotropical migrant birds in fragmented forests of Illinois was extremely low due to high predation rates and brood parasitism by brown-headed cowbirds (Robinson 1990). Newmark (1991) reported local extinctions of forest interior birds in Tanzania due to fragmentation of tropical forests. Fragmentation of wetlands is an important issue for wildlife managers to address. Some useful references on fragmentation relative to forest birds are Askins et al. (1987), Robbins et al. (1989), Freemark and Merriam (1986), and Freemark and Collins (1992). The latter study includes a list of area-sensitive or forest interior birds for the eastern United States. The work of Robbins et al. (1989) is particularly relevant to the Northeast as they addressed area requirements of forest birds in the Mid-Atlantic states. They found that species such as the black-throated blue warbler, cerulean warbler, Canada warbler, and black-and-white warbler required very large tracts of forest for breeding. Table 1 lists some area-sensitive birds for the region. Ground-nesters, such as veery, black-and-white warbler, worm-eating warbler, ovenbird, waterthrushes, and Kentucky warbler, are particularly sensitive to predation which may be increased in fragmented landscapes. Robbins et al. (1989) suggest a minimum forest size of 7,410 acres to retain all species of the forest-breeding avifauna in the Mid-Atlantic region.

The analysis identifies two basic wetland types with potential for providing highly significant habitat for other wildlife: 1) large wetlands ($\geq$ 20 acres) regardless of vegetative cover but excluding pine plantations, and 2) smaller diverse wetlands (10-20 acres with multiple cover types). These two categories cover most wetlands along stream corridors that connect large wetland complexes. In addition to these wetlands, large clusters of small wetlands located within a forest matrix are also recognized as having high potential for wildlife habitat as well as vegetated wetlands connected to other vegetated wetlands by forests. The remaining vegetated wetlands are designated as having moderate potential significance for providing wildlife habitat.

Please note that in general, ponds are not listed as important as significant for "other wildlife." Wildlife species living in ponds, such as several species of frogs and turtles, are mentioned in the discussion of fish and shellfish habitat, since wetlands designated as important for fish and shellfish are provide required habitat for these species.

| | High | Large vegetated wetlands (≥20 acres, excluding open water, nonvegetated areas, and pine plantations), small diverse wetlands (10-20 acres with 2 or more covertypes; excluding EM5 or open water as one of the covertypes), areas with large numbers of small isolated wetlands (within an upland forest matrix and including small ponds that may be vernal pools) |
| | Moderate | Other vegetated wetlands |

Given the general nature of this assessment of "other wildlife habitat," other individuals may want to refine this assessment in the future by having biologists designate "target species" that may be used to identify important wildlife habitats in a particular watershed. After doing this, they could identify criteria that may be used to identify potentially significant habitat for these species in the watershed. Dr. Hank Short (U.S. Fish and Wildlife Service, retired) compiled a matrix listing 332 species of wildlife and their likely occurrence in wetlands of various types in New England from ECOSEARCH models (Short et al. 1996) that he developed with Dr. Dick DeGraaf (U.S. Forest Service) and Dr. Jay Hestbeck (U.S. Fish and Wildlife Service).[3] DeGraaf and Rudis (1986) summarized habitat, natural history, and distribution of New England wildlife. Much of what is in the ECOSEARCH models comes from this source. These sources may be useful starting points for determining relationships between wildlife and wetlands.

---

[3]Copies of the matrix can be obtained by contacting R. Tiner (address on title page).

Table 1. List of some area-sensitive birds for forests of the Mid-Atlantic region. (Source: Robbins et al. 1989).

Species	Area (acres) at which probability of occurrence is reduced by 50%
Neotropical Migrants	
Acadian flycatcher	37
Blue-gray gnatcatcher	37
Veery	49
Northern parula	1,280
Black-throated blue warbler	2,500
Cerulean warbler	1,700
Black-and-white warbler	543
Worm-eating warbler	370
Ovenbird	15
Northern waterthrush	494
Louisiana waterthrush	865
Canada warbler	988
Summer tanager	99
Scarlet tanager	30
Short-distance Migrants	
Red-shouldered hawk	556
Permanent Residents	
Hairy woodpecker	17
Pileated woodpecker	408

Conservation of Biodiversity

In the context of this assessment, the term "biodiversity" is used to identify wetlands that may contribute to the preservation of an assemblage of wetlands that encompass the natural diversity of wetlands in a given watershed. Four types of wetlands may be identified: 1) certain wetland types that appear to be scarce or relatively uncommon in the watershed, 2) individual wetlands that possess several different covertypes (i.e., naturally diverse wetland complexes), 3) complexes of large wetlands, and 4) regionally unique or uncommon wetland types. The first two categories may include some wetlands that are human-impacted (e.g., impounded, excavated, timber harvested) or created; they support an uncommon wetland type and have been included as significant from our broad perspective. Some investigators may not consider such wetlands to be worth highlighting for "biodiversity" because they are the result of human actions and may not be viewed as reflecting "natural" conditions. Users can make their own decisions on how to regard these findings.

Schroeder (1996) noted that to conserve regional biodiversity, maintenance of large-area habitats for forest interior birds is essential. As mentioned previously, Robbins et al. (1989) suggest a minimum forest size of 7,410 acres to retain all species of the forest-breeding avifauna in the Mid-Atlantic region. Consequently, forested areas 7,410 acres and larger that contained contiguous palustrine forested wetlands and upland forests were designated as important for maintaining regional biodiversity of avifauna in the Mid-Atlantic Region based on recommendations by Robbins et al. (1989). This criterion will be applied throughout the Northeast as no comparable data are available for other areas of the region. A few large wetlands in a watershed (e.g., possibly important for interior nesting birds and wide-ranging wildlife in general) and wetlands that are uncommon types (based on NWI mapping classification and not on Natural Heritage Program data) may also be identified as significant for biodiversity. The size of the "large" wetlands is variable depending on the distribution of size classes in a watershed, but they should typically be larger than 100 acres. All riverine and palustrine tidal wetlands and estuarine oligohaline vegetated wetlands are identified as significant for this function because they are often possess some of the most diverse wetland plant communities in the Northeast. We also identified other specific wetland types of particular interest to biodiversity. Phragmites-dominated wetlands are generally excluded from the listing except in urban areas where large stands (e.g., New Jersey Meadowlands) are recognized as significant natural habitats.

Use of Natural Heritage Program data and GAP data have been suggested, but use of these data are beyond the scope of our remotely sensed approach to wetland functional analysis. Consequently, wetlands designated as potentially significant for biodiversity by the W-PAWF assessment are simply a starting point or a foundation to build upon. Local knowledge of significant wetlands and Natural Heritage Program data can be applied by others to further refine the list of wetlands important for this function for specific geographic areas.

The following are examples of wetlands viewed as potentially significant for the conservation of biodiversity in the Northeast:

Regionally
Significant

Estuarine oligohaline vegetated wetlands (excluding Phragmites-dominated)
Riverine tidal emergent wetlands (including tidal flats that are often colonized by nonpersistent plants during the growing season)
Palustrine tidal emergent wetlands (excluding Phragmites-dominated)
Palustrine tidal scrub-shrub wetlands
Atlantic white cedar swamps
Calcareous fens
Bald cypress swamps
Eelgrass beds
Lotic fringe wetlands
Areas with clusters of vernal pools
Headwater seep wetlands?
Rare plant habitats
Forested wetland-forested upland complexes >7410 acres in size

Locally
Significant
(possibly)

Urban wetlands
Shrub bogs
Mussel reefs
Oyster reefs
Larch swamps
Northern white cedar swamps
Hemlock swamps
Estuarine emergent wetlands (some areas)
Lentic fringe wetlands (EM/AB and AB/EM wetlands)
Uncommon types based on Inventory results

Summary

The U.S. Fish and Wildlife Service is attempting to add descriptors for landscape position, landform, and water flow path to its wetland digital database in the Northeast when updating NWI maps and digital data. When combined with typical NWI attributes from Cowardin et al. 1979 (system, subsystem, class, subclass, water regime, and special modifiers), the database contains many properties for each wetland that can be used to produce a preliminary assessment of wetland functions for large geographic areas. The focus of these analyses is on watersheds which are important land planning units for a number of agencies and organizations, but the same procedures can be applied to other land units such as counties or physiographic regions. The subject report provides the rationale for the criteria used to identify wetlands of potential significance for ten functions. These functions include: 1) surface water detention, 2) coastal storm surge detention, 3) streamflow maintenance, 4) nutrient transformation, 5) sediment and other particulate retention, 6) shoreline stabilization, 7) provision of fish and shellfish habitat, 8) provision of waterfowl and waterbird habitat, 9) provision of other wildlife habitat, and 10) conservation of biodiversity.

Acknowledgments

Many people had a hand in developing these correlations over the past five years. During this period, various iterations of these correlations were used to identify potential wetlands of significance for the specified functions in several watershed assessment studies. These studies were conducted in Maine, New York, Pennsylvania, Delaware, and Maryland. The present document reflects input from the numerous individuals including: Dan Arsenault, Matt Schweisberg, and Doug Thompson (U.S. Environmental Protection Agency, Region I), Bob Houston and Stewart Fefer (U.S. Fish & Wildlife Service, Gulf of Maine Office), Jay Clement and Christine Godfrey (U.S. Army Corps of Engineers, New England District), Jeanne Difranco, Alison Ward, and Don Witherall (Maine Department of Environmental Protection), Ken Elowe, Francis Brautigam, Sandy Eldridge, and Phil Bozenhard (Maine Department of Inland Fisheries and Wildlife), Betty McInnes (Cumberland County Soil and Water Conservation District, Maine), Katherine Goves (Casco Bay Estuary Project), Andy Cutko (Maine Natural Areas Program), Marcia Spencer-Famous (Maine Land Use Regulation Commission), Bob Bistrais (Maine Office of GIS), Wende Mahaney (U.S. Fish and Wildlife Service, Maine Field Office), Eugenie Moore and Steve Pelletier (Woodlot Alternatives), (U.S. Environmental Protection Agency, Region I), Mike Bartlett and Bill Neidermyer (U.S. Fish & Wildlife Service, New England Field Office), Jackie Sartoris and Liz Hertz (Maine State Planning Office), Dr. Jerry Longcore (U.S. Geological Survey, Biological Resources Division), Dr. Christopher Pennuto (University of Southern Maine), Dr. Hank Short (U.S. Fish & Wildlife Service, Northeast Region), Laurie Machung (New York City Department of Environmental Protection), Amy Jacobs and Mark Biddle (Delaware Department of Natural Resources and Environmental Control), David Bleil, Katheleen Freeman, Cathy Wazniak, Mitch Keiler, and Bill Jenkins (Maryland Department of Natural Resources), Julie LaBranche (Maryland Department of the Environment), Marcia Snyder, Dr. Dennis Whigham, and Dr. Don Weller (Smithsonian Environmental Research Center, Edgewater, Maryland), Dr. Matt Perry and Jon Willow (U.S. Geological Survey, Biological Resources Division), Peter Bowman (Delaware Natural Heritage Program), Nicholas Staats (U.S. Fish and Wildlife Service, Lake Champlain Fish and Wildlife Resources Office), Dr. Arthur Gold (University of Rhode Island), and George Haas (U.S. Fish & Wildlife Service, Regional Migratory Bird Coordinator). Their contributions to this effort are greatly appreciated.

References

Askins, R.A., M.J. Philbrick, and D.S. Sugeno. 1987. Relationship between the regional abundance of forest and the composition of forest bird communities. Biol. Cons. 39: 129-152.

Bowden, W.B. 1987. The biogeochemistry of nitrogen in freshwater wetlands. Biogeochemistry 4: 313-348.

Brinson, M. M. 1993a. A Hydrogeomorphic Classification for Wetlands. U.S. Army Corps of Engineers, Washington, DC. Wetlands Research Program, Technical Report WRP-DE-4.

Brinson, M.M. 1993b. Changes in the functioning of wetlands along environmental gradients. Wetlands 13; 65-74.

Buresh, R.J., M.E. Casselman, and W.H. Patrick. 1980. Nitrogen fixation in flooded soil systems, a review. Advances in Agronomy 33: 149-192.

Carter, V. 1996. Wetland hydrology, water quality, and associated functions. In: J.D. Fretwell, J.S. Williams, and P.J. Redman (compilers). National Water Summary on Wetland Resources. U.S. Geological Survey, Reston, VA. Water-Supply Paper 2425. pp. 35-48.

Cowardin, L. M., V. Carter, F. C. Golet, and E. T. LaRoe. 1979. Classification of Wetlands and Deepwater Habitats of the United States. U.S. Fish and Wildlife Service, Washington, DC. FWS/OBS-79/31.

DeGraaf, R.M. and D.D. Rudis. 1986. New England Wildlife: Habitat, Natural History, and Distribution. U.S.D.A. Forest Service, Northeastern Forest Expt. Station, Amherst, MA. Gen. Tech. Rep. NE-108.

DeLaune, R.D., R.R. Boar, C.W. Lindau, and B.A. Kleiss. 1996. Denitrification in bottomland hardwood wetland soils of the Cache River. Wetlands 16: 309-320.

Freemark, K. and B. Collins. 1992. Landscape ecology of breeding birds in temperate forest fragments. In: J.W. Hagan III and D.W. Johnston (editors). Ecology and Conservation of Neotropical Birds. Smithsonian Institution Press. pp. 443-453.

Freemark, K.E. and H.G. Merriam. 1986. Importance of area and habitat heterogenity to bird assemblages in temperate forest fragments. Biol. Cons. 36: 115-141.

Golet, F.C. 1972. Classification and Evaluation of Freshwater Wetlands as Wildlife Habitat in the Glaciated Northeast. University of Massachusetts, Amherst, MA. Ph. D. dissertation.

Hammer, D.A. 1992. Creating Freshwater Wetlands. Lewis Publishers, Inc., Chelsea, MI.

Matsuguchi, T. 1979. In: Nitrogen and Rice. International Rice Research Institute, Los Banos, Philippines. Pp. 207-222.

Mitsch, W.J. and J.G. Gosselink. 2000. Wetlands. Van Nostrand Reinhold, New York, NY.

Nelson, W.M., A.J. Gold, and P.M. Groffman. 1995. Spatial and temporal variation in groundwater nitrate removal in a riparian forest. J. Environ. Qual. 24; 691-699.

Newmark, W.D. 1991. Tropical forest fragmentation and the local extinction of understory birds in the eastern Usambara Mountains, Tanzania. Conservation Biology 5: 67-78.

Novitzki, R.P. 1979. The hydrologic characteristics of Wisconsin wetlands and their influence on floods, streamflow, and sediment. In: P.E. Greeson et al. (editors). Wetland Functions and Values: The State of Our Understanding. Amer. Water Resources Assoc., Minneapolis, MN. pp. 377-388.

Patrick, W.H., Jr. undated. Microbial reactions of nitrogen and phosphorus in wetlands. The Utrecht Plant Ecology News Report No. 11 (10): 52-63.

Patrick, W.H., Jr., and R.A. Khalid. 1974. Phosphate release and sorption by soils and sediments: effect of aerobic and anaerobic conditions. Science 186: 53-55.

Peterjohn, W.T. and D.L. Correll. 1982. Nutrient dynamics in an agricultural watershed: observations on the role of a riparian forest. Ecology 65: 1466-1475.

Robbins, C.S., D.K. Dawson, and B.A. Dowell. 1989. Habitat area requirements of breeding forest birds of the Mid-Atlantic states. Wildlife Monogr. 103: 1-34.

Robinson, S.K. 1990. Effects of Forest Fragmentation on Nesting Songbirds. Illinois Natural History Survey, Champaign, IL.

Schroeder, R.L. 1996. Wildlife Community Habitat Evaluation Using a Modified Species-Area Relationship. U.S. Army Corps of Engineers, Waterways Expt. Station, Vicksburg, MS. Wetlands Research Program Tech. Rep. WRP-DE-12.

Short, H. L., J. B. Hestbeck, and R. W. Tiner. 1996. Ecosearch: a new paradigm for evaluating the utility of wildlife habitat. In: Conservation of Faunal Diversity in Forested Landscapes. R. M. DeGraaf and R. L. Miller (editors). Chapman & Hall, London. pp. 569-594.

Simmons, R.C., A.J. Gold, and P.M. Groffman. 1992. Nitrate dynamics in riparian forests: groundwater studies. J. Environ. Qual. 21: 659-665.

Simpson, R.L., R.E. Good, R. Walker, and B.R. Frasco. 1983. The role of Delaware River freshwater tidal wetlands in the retention of nutrients and heavy metals. J. Environ. Qual. 12: 41-48.

Tiner, R.W. 1995. A landscape and landform classification for Northeast wetlands (an operational draft). U.S. Fish and Wildlife Service, Ecological Services, Northeast Region, Hadley, MA.

Tiner, R.W. 1996a. A landscape and landform classification for Northeast wetlands. U..S. Fish and Wildlife Service, National Wetlands Inventory Project, Northeast Region, Hadley, MA.

Tiner, R.W. 1996b. Keys to landscape position and landform descriptors for Northeast wetlands. U.S. Fish and Wildlife Service, Ecological Services, Northeast Region, Hadley, MA.

Tiner, R.W. 1997a. Keys to landscape position and landform descriptors fo U.S. wetlands (operational draft). U.S. Fish and Wildlife Service, National Wetlands Inventory Program, Northeast Region, Hadley, MA.

Tiner, R.W. 1997b. Piloting a more descriptive NWI. National Wetlands Newsletter 19(5): 14-16.

Tiner, R.W. 1997c. NWI Maps: What They Tell Us. National Wetlands Newsletter 19(2): 7-12. (Copy available from USFWS, ES-NWI, 300 Westgate Center Drive, Hadley, MA 01035)

Tiner, R.W. 1998. In Search of Swampland: A Wetland Sourcebook and Field Guide. Rutgers University Press, New Brunswick, NJ.

Tiner, R.W. 1999. Wetland Indicators: A Guide to Wetland Identification, Delineation, Classification, and Mapping. Lewis Publishers, CRC Press, Boca Raton, FL.

Tiner, R. W. 2000. Keys to Waterbody Type and Hydrogeomorphic-type Wetland Descriptors for U.S. Waters and Wetlands (Operational Draft). U.S. Fish and Wildlife Service, Northeast Region, Hadley, MA.

Tiner, R. W. 2002. Keys to Waterbody Type and Hydrogeomorphic-type Wetland Descriptors for U.S. Waters and Wetlands (Operational Draft). U.S. Fish and Wildlife Service, Northeast Region, Hadley, MA.

Tiner, R.W. 2003. Illustrated Keys and Mapping Codes for Application of Wetland Landscape Position, Landform, Water Flow Path, and Waterbody Type Descriptors in the United States. Draft report.

Tiner, R.W. and G. DeAlessio. 2002. Wetlands of Pennsylvania's Coastal Zone: Wetland Status, Preliminary Functional Assessment, and Recent Trends (1986-1999). U.S. Fish and Wildlife Service, National Wetlands Inventory Program, Northeast Region, Hadley, MA.

Tiner, R., S. Schaller, D. Peterson, K. Snider, K. Ruhlman, and J. Swords. 1999. Wetland Characterization Study and Preliminary Assessment of Wetland Functions for the Casco Bay

Watershed, Southern Maine. U.S. Fish and Wildlife Service, Northeast Region, NWI-ES, Hadley, MA.

Tiner, R., M. Starr, H. Bergquist, and J. Swords. 2000. Watershed-based Wetland Characterization for Maryland's Nanticoke River and Coastal Bays Watersheds: A Preliminary Assessment Report. U.S. Fish and Wildlife Service, National Wetlands Inventory Program, Ecological Services, Northeast Region, Hadley, MA. (on web listed under publications at: http://wetlands.fws.gov)

Tiner, R.W., H.C. Bergquist, J.Q. Swords, and B.J. McClain. 2001. Watershed-based Wetland Characterization for Delaware's Nanticoke River Watershed: A Preliminary Assessment Report. U.S. Fish and Wildlife Service, National Wetlands Inventory Program, Ecological Services, Northeast Region, Hadley, MA.

Tiner, R.W., H.C. Bergquist, and B.J. McClain. 2002. Wetland Characterization and Preliminary Assessment of Wetland Functions for the Neversink Reservoir and Cannonsville Reservoir Basins of the New York City Water Supply Watershed. U.S. Fish and Wildlife Service, National Wetlands Inventory Program, Ecological Services, Northeast Region, Hadley, MA.

U.S. Fish and Wildlife Service. 2003. Gulf of Maine Watershed Habitat Analysis. Version 3.1. Gulf of Maine Coastal Program Office, Falmouth, MA. (http://gulfofmaine.fws.gov)

Wada, H., S. Panichsakpatana, M. Kimura, and Y. Takai. 1978. Soil Sci. Plant Nutr. 24: 357-365.

Wang, L., J. Lyons, P. Kanehl, and R.Gatti. 1997. Influences of watershed land use on habitat quality and biotic integrity of Wisconsin streams. Fisheries 22(6): 6-12.

Whigham, D.F., C. Chitterling, and B. Palmer. 1988. Impacts of freshwater wetlands on water quality: a landscape perspective. Environ. Manag. 12: 663-671.

Whiting, P.J. 1998. Bank storage and its influence on streamflow. Stream Notes July 1998. Stream Systems Technology Center, Rocky Mountain Research Station, Fort Collins, CO.

Yarbro, L.A., E.J. Kuenzler, P.J. Mulholland, and R.P. Sniffen. 1984. Effects of stream channelization on exports of nitrogen and phosphorus from North Carolina Coastal Plain watersheds. Environ. Manag. 8: 151-160.